Program Authors

Peter Afflerbach	Jeanne Paratore
Camille Blachowicz	P. David Pearson
Candy Dawson Boyd	Sam Sebesta
Wendy Cheyney	Deborah Simmons
Connie Juel	Sharon Vaughn
Edward Kame'enui	Susan Watts-Taffe
Donald Leu	Karen Kring Wixson

PEARSON

Scott Foresman

Editorial Offices: Glenview, Illinois • Parsippany, New Jersey • New York, New York
Sales Offices: Needham, Massachusetts • Duluth, Georgia • Glenview, Illinois
Coppell, Texas • Sacramento, California • Mesa, Arizona

We dedicate Reading Street to
Peter Jovanovich.

His wisdom, courage,
and passion for education
are an inspiration to us all.

About the Cover Artist

Daniel Moreton lives in New York City, where he uses his computer to create illustrations for books. When he is not working, Daniel enjoys cooking, watching movies, and traveling. On a trip to Mexico, Daniel was inspired by all of the bright colors around him. He likes to use those colors in his art.

ISBN: 0-328-10832-4

4 5 6 7 8 9 10 V063 14 13 12 11 10 09 08 07 06

Dear Reader,

Scott Foresman Reading Street has many corners and crossroads. At each corner you will learn about something new and interesting. You will read about great ideas in science and social studies. You will have fun reading about clever chicks and smart mice detectives!

You may want to hurry down the street and read these wonderful stories and articles! But slow down, take your time, and enjoy yourself! You never know who you might meet on *Reading Street!*

Sincerely,
The Authors

Great Ideas

What difference can a great idea make?

Clever Solutions

Unit Opener 8

Let's Talk About Clever Solutions 10

Words to Read 12

animal fantasy
Tippy-Toe Chick, Go! 14
by George Shannon
illustrated by Laura Dronzek

fable
Belling the Cat 36
adapted from a fable by Aesop
illustrated by Viviana Garofoli

Language Arts: Commands 42

Let's Talk About Clever Solutions 44

Words to Read. 46

animal fantasy/social studies

Mole and the Baby Bird . . . 48

by Marjorie Newman
illustrated by Patrick Benson

jokes/social studies

Dear Dr. Know-It-All 68

by Paulinda Lynk

Language Arts: Exclamations 74

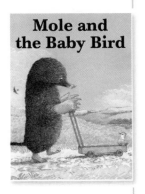

Let's Talk About Clever Solutions 76

Words to Read. 78

informational fiction/science

Dot & Jabber and the Great Acorn Mystery . . 80

by Ellen Stoll Walsh

expository nonfiction/science

Water 104

Language Arts: How Sentences Begin and End. . . . 108

Ideas That Changed the World

Let's Talk About Ideas That Changed the World. . .110

Words to Read. 112

expository nonfiction/science
Simple Machines 114
by Allan Fowler

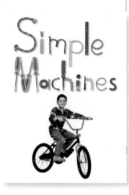

narrative nonfiction/science
Roy's Wheelchair 134
by Callen Watkins

Language Arts: Pronouns. 138

Let's Talk About Ideas That Changed the World. . .140

Words to Read. 142

biography/social studies
Alexander Graham Bell. . .144
by Lola M. Schaefer

web site/social studies online
Inventions 166

Language Arts: Using I and Me 168

Let's Talk About Ideas That Changed the World. . . 170

Words to Read. 172

biography/social studies
Ben Franklin and His First Kite. 174
by Stephen Krensky
illustrated by Bert Dodson

poetry
Poetry Collection 198
I Made a Mechanical Dragon by Jack Prelutsky
illustrated by Peter Sis

Lighthouse by Joan Bransfield Graham
illustrated by Nancy Davis

Language Arts: More About Pronouns 202

Unit Wrap-Up 204

Question and Answer Strategies 206

Glossary 210

Tested Words List. 220

Great Ideas

What difference can a great idea make?

connect to
SOCIAL STUDIES

Tippy-Toe Chick, Go!

Little Chick solves a big problem.

ANIMAL FANTASY

connect to
SOCIAL STUDIES

Mole and the Baby Bird

Grandfather helps Mole see his pet in a new way.

ANIMAL FANTASY

connect to
SCIENCE

Dot & Jabber and the Great Acorn Mystery

Dot and Jabber solve a science mystery.

INFORMATIONAL FICTION

connect to
SCIENCE

Simple Machines

We learn how simple machines make our lives easier.

EXPOSITORY NONFICTION

connect to
SOCIAL STUDIES

Alexander Graham Bell

Alexander Graham Bell's invention improved how we communicate.

BIOGRAPHY

connect to
SOCIAL STUDIES

Ben Franklin and His First Kite

One great idea can lead to another.

BIOGRAPHY

9

Let's Talk About
Clever Solutions

Words to Read

along
behind
toward
eyes
never
pulling

Read the Words

The chicks walked along the path behind the house. They walked toward the garden. Their eyes popped open! They saw a big dog that they had never seen before. It was barking and pulling on its leash.

Tippy-Toe Chick, GO!

Genre: Animal Fantasy
The animal characters in an animal fantasy act like people. In the next story you will read about a smart little chick who surprises her family.

Tippy-Toe

by George Shannon

illustrated by Laura Dronzek

Chick, GO!

What great idea
will Little Chick have?

Every morning when the dew had dried, Hen took her chicks to the garden for their favorite treat—sweet itty-bitty beans and potato bugs.

Hen, Big Chick, and Middle Chick next, with Little Chick trailing along behind. Stopping to wonder at this and that.

Then running, *tippy-toe, tippy-toe,* to
catch the rest. Across the yard. Into the
garden to eat, eat, eat. Every day, every day
of the week.

Till ONE day—

RUFF-RUFF-RUFF-RUFF-RUFF!

A big, grumpy dog came running their way, barking and growling at the end of a rope.

Hen jumped back and pulled her chicks near. "There's no safe way to the beans today. We'll just have to wait for chicken feed."

All three chicks said, "Bleck!" and frowned.

"We're hungry!"

"You PROMISED!"

"We DID our chores!"

Hen sighed. "But we'll NEVER get past a dog like that."

Big Chick said, "Wait. I'LL take care of this."
He slowly took a step toward Dog. "Now listen,"
he called. "We won't hurt you. We're just going
to the garden for an itty-bitty treat."

RUFF-RUFF-RUFF-RUFF-RUFF!

Dog disagreed, barking and pulling at the end of his rope. Big Chick ran to hide under Hen's safe wing.

Middle Chick took a breath, then stepped toward Dog. "I'M hungry, so YOU'D better stop it right now! Or YOU'LL be sorry when we get hold of you."

RUFF-RUFF-RUFF-RUFF-RUFF!

Dog disagreed, barking and pulling at the end
of his rope. Middle Chick ran to hide under
Hen's safe wing.

"Let's go," said Hen. "We'll really have to wait."

Little Chick peeped, "*I* want to try."

"Oh, no!" said Hen, as the other chicks laughed. "You're much too small."

Little Chick yelled, "But *I* can RUN!" And off she went, *tippy-toe, tippy-toe,* as fast as she could. Straight toward Dog.

Hen screamed and grabbed her heart.

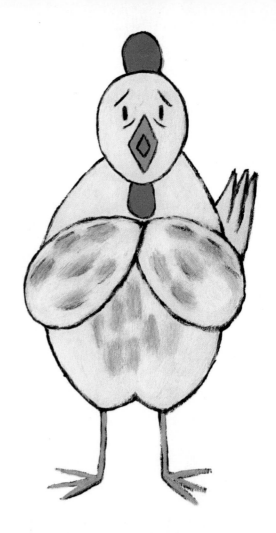

Big Chick closed his eyes.

Middle Chick shook.

Little Chick ran, *tippy-toe, tippy-toe*, without stopping to rest till she felt Dog's breath.

Then Little Chick laughed and began to run again. *Tippy-toe, tippy-toe* around the tree.

Dog chased after her, tugging at his rope.
RUFF-RUFF-RUFF-RUFF-RUFF!

Tippy-toe, tippy-toe around the tree. *Tippy-toe, tippy-toe, tippy* . . . **RUFF-RUFF-RUFF!**

Around and around, *tippy-toe, tippy-toe.* Till . . .

RUFF-RUP-yip-yip-yip-yip!

Dog's rope was wrapped all around the tree.
He was stuck and too mad to think "back up."

Hen clucked with pride. Big Chick and Middle
Chick just stood and stared.

Little Chick called, "It's time to eat!"

And off they ran, *tippy-toe, tippy-toe.* Right past Dog and into the garden for their favorite treat—sweet itty-bitty beans and potato bugs.

"YUM!"

Think and Share

Talk About It What would you say to Little Chick about her great idea?

1. The pictures below are mixed up. Decide in which order they belong. Then use them to retell the story.

2. Where does Little Chick live? What words would you use to describe her?

3. What happened to Little Chick and her family at the beginning of the story? What happened at the end?

Look Back and Write Why was Little Chick's idea great? Look at pages 28–31.

Meet the Author
George Shannon

George Shannon is a tall man, but he likes little things. One of his favorite sayings is "Less is more." Does that sound like a good lesson for Little Chick?

Mr. Shannon likes to tell stories. He says, "I want my stories to sound as if they are being told out loud."

Read more books by George Shannon.

35

Belling the Cat

a fable adapted from Aesop
illustrated by Viviana Garofoli

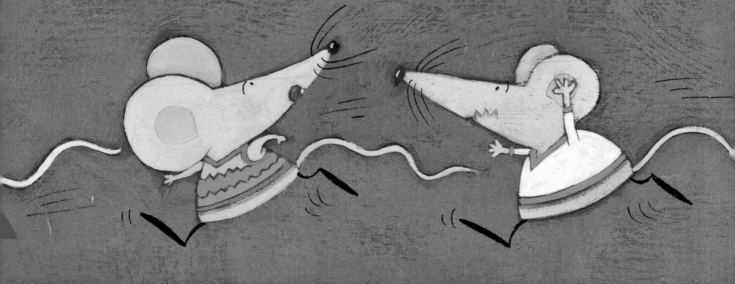

The mice had a problem. There was a new
cat in the house. It slept by the kitchen table.
It hid behind doors. It raced down the hall
toward the mice.

They could see its eyes in the dark.
They could hear it howl at night. They never
felt safe!

The mice called a meeting. They had many ideas.

One little mouse pulled on his ear and said, "We need to hear that cat. Let's hang a bell on its neck."

All the mice went along with the idea.
They cheered and clapped. They danced
and laughed.

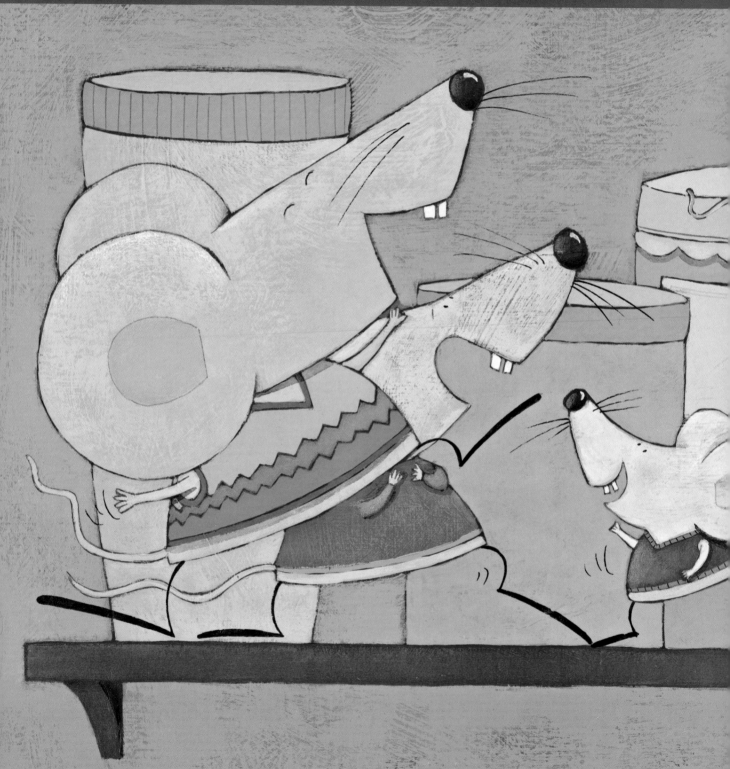

Then a wise old mouse asked, "Who is going to bell the cat?"

Moral: Some things are easier said than done.

Read Together

Commands

A **command** is a sentence that
tells someone to do something.
It begins with a capital letter.
It ends with a **period (.)**.

Come back, Little Chick**.**

Please go away, Dog**.**

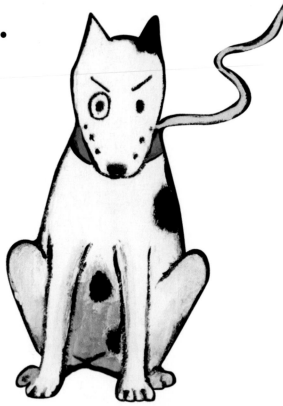

Write Using Commands

1. Read these sentences. Write the sentence that is a command.

The big dog growled.
Run fast.

2. Write these sentences again. Make them commands. Use capital letters and periods.

Will you please do your chores now?
Will you walk the dog?

3. Imagine you are training your dog. Write commands telling your dog what to do. Use capital letters and periods.

Let's Talk About

Clever Solutions

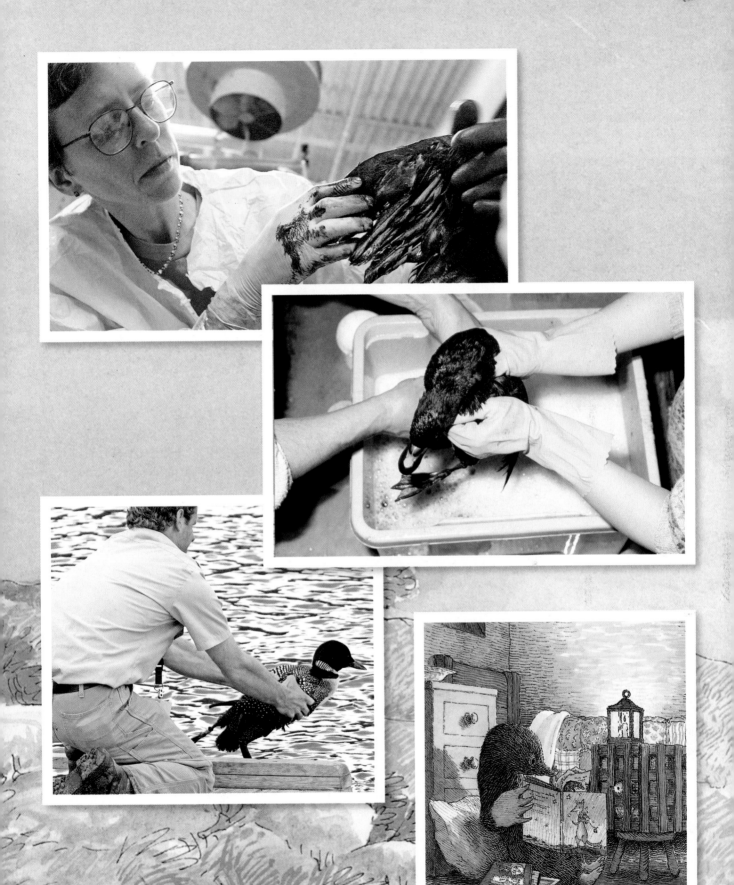

Words to Read

loved
wood
should
door

Read the Words

Mole loved the baby bird he found. He put it in a cage made of wood. What should Mole do? Should he keep the baby bird, or should he open the cage door and let the bird go?

Mole and the Baby Bird

Genre: Animal Fantasy

In an animal fantasy, the animal characters talk and act like people. The next story is about a mole who finds and takes care of a wild bird.

Mole and
the Baby Bird

by Marjorie Newman

illustrated by Patrick Benson

*What can Mole learn
from a baby bird?*

49

Mole found a baby bird.
It had fallen out of its nest.

Mole waited and waited: but no
big bird came to help it–so Mole
took the baby bird home.

He made a nest for it.
"Look!" he said to his mother.

"It's very, very hard to take care of a baby
bird," she said.

"They usually die," said his dad.

"My bird won't die," said Mole.

His friends helped him find food
for the baby.

His mother showed him how to feed it.
Mole fed it whenever it chirped.

And the bird didn't die! It grew.
"It's my pet bird," said Mole.
"It's not a pet bird. It's a wild bird,"
said his mother.

The bird fluttered its wings.

"Your bird is trying to fly," said his mother.

"No!" cried Mole. "It mustn't fly!"

Mole found some wood and some nails.
He borrowed his dad's toolbox.

"What are you making?" asked his dad.
"I'm making a cage for my pet bird!"
said Mole.

"It's not a pet bird. It's a wild bird,"
said his dad. "You should let it fly."
"No!" cried Mole.

He put his bird into its new cage.
The bird was sad.

Mole's mother was sad too. But Mole
kept his bird, because he loved it.

Then—Grandad came to visit. He looked at
Mole's pet bird.

Presently Grandad said, "Let's go for a walk,
little Mole."

Grandad took Mole to the top of a high hill.

Mole looked down at the trees far below.

He felt the wild wind trying to lift him.
"Wheee! I'm flying!" cried Mole.
"Nearly," said Grandad.

When Mole got home he looked at his bird.
It was sitting very still in its cage in Mole's dark
underground room. "Birds are meant to fly,"
said Mole.

He opened the cage door, and he let his bird
fly away because he loved it. Then he cried.

The next day Mole went into the forest.
He saw his bird flying, soaring, free. And Mole
was glad.

Think and Share

Talk About It What lesson did Mole learn? Was it a good lesson to learn? Why do you think so?

1. Use the pictures below to retell the story of *Mole and the Baby Bird.*

2. Tell two things that happened after Mole found the baby bird.

3. How did Mole change at the end of the story?

Look Back and Write Mole tries to treat the baby bird like a pet. Look back at the story. What did he do? Make a list.

Marjorie Newman

Marjorie Newman lives in England.
As a child, she often brought
home caterpillars and tadpoles.
When they turned into butterflies
and frogs, she let them go.

Patrick Benson

Patrick Benson tries to show
different views in his art. Can you
find a picture that shows how the
world looks to a flying bird?

**Read another book
by Marjorie Newman or
illustrated by Patrick Benson.**

Dear Dr. Know-It-All

by Paulinda Lynk

Dear Dr. Know-It-All,
My sister never knocks on my door. She just barges into my room. What should I do?
Getting Mad

68

Dear Getting Mad:
Tape a knock-knock joke to the wood on your door. Your sister will stop and read it! After that, I bet she will knock.
Dr. Know-It-All

Dear Dr. Know-It-All,
I loved your idea!
And it worked.
I even found a book
of knock-knock jokes
to keep her knocking!
Not Mad Now

Knock! Knock!
Who's There?
Boo.
Boo who?
Why are you crying?

More Knock-knock Jokes

Knock-Knock

Knock-knock.
Who's there?
Orange.
Orange who?
Orange you glad to see me?

Knock-knock.
Who's there?
Olive.
Olive who?
Olive to play with you!

Knock-knock.
Who's there?
Who.
Who who?
When did you get an owl?

Knock-knock.
Who's there?
Les.
Les who?
Les be friends!

Exclamations

An **exclamation** is a sentence that shows strong feeling. It begins with a **capital letter.** It ends with an exclamation mark **(!).**

Mole has strong feelings about the baby bird. He wants to keep it. How would Mole say this sentence?

"**I**t mustn't fly**!**" cried Mole.

Write Using Exclamations

1. Write these exclamations. Use capital letters and exclamation marks correctly.

we love our pet bird
our bird just fell out of its nest

· ·

2. Look in *Mole and the Baby Bird*. Find another sentence that is an exclamation. Write it.

· ·

3. Choose a kind of bird. Write about it. Use some exclamations.

Let's Talk About
Clever
Solutions

	Taste	Touch	Smell	What is it?
Object 1	sour	bumpy		
Object 2				
Object 3				

?

Words to Read

among
instead
another
none

Read the Words

    We looked outside. A squirrel found an acorn among the leaves. He didn't eat it. Instead, he dug a hole and put the acorn in it. Then the squirrel found another acorn. None of us saw where he put that one.

Dot & Jabber
and the Great Acorn Mystery

Genre: Informational Fiction
Informational fiction tells a make-believe story, but it also gives facts and information that are true. The next story is a mystery about trees and how they grow where they do.

Dot & Jabber
and the Great Acorn Mystery

by Ellen Stoll Walsh

How will Dot and Jabber

solve this mystery?

The detectives had nothing to do.

"We need a mystery to solve," said Jabber.

"Here's a mystery," said Dot. "What is this little oak tree doing here?"

"Why is that a mystery?" Jabber wanted
to know.

"Because of the acorn," said Dot. "How did
it get here?"

"Dot," said Jabber, "what acorn?"

"Acorns are oak tree seeds. This little oak tree grew from an acorn, and acorns come from big oak trees."

"Oh, *that* acorn," said Jabber. "But where's the big oak tree?"

"That's part of the mystery," said Dot. "Let's look for clues."

"Okay!" shouted Jabber. "Because we're detectives!" He poked his head into a hole.

"Hey, this is *my* hole," said a mole. "Go away. There are no clues down here. Try the big oak tree—on the *other* side of the meadow."

"Of course!" said Dot. "Come on, Jabber!"

"That's a long, long way," said Jabber.
"How did our acorn get from there to here?
Do you think it walked?"

"Let's find out," said Dot. "The acorn began at the big oak tree. So will we."
The detectives set off across the meadow.

After a while Jabber said, "I'm tired. Can we wonder about all these maple seeds instead?"

"There's no mystery in maple seeds," said Dot. "They have wings that twirl, and they ride the wind across the meadow."

"Maybe our acorn rode the wind too,"
said Jabber.

"That is what we are going to find out,"
said Dot.

At last they arrived at the big oak tree. "Look!" said Dot. "I bet there are a million acorns here."

"They don't have wings," said Jabber.
"But they taste good."
"Don't eat them, Jabber! They're clues."

"Acorns don't have wings, but they might
have sneaky feet," said Dot. "Let's keep watch
and see if they start to move."

Plip. An acorn dropped from the big oak tree.

Jabber poked it with a stick. "This acorn isn't going anywhere," he said. "None of them are."

A squirrel came and sat down among
the acorns.

"Jabber, look!" Dot whispered. "What is
he doing?"

"Oh!" gasped Jabber. "He's eating our clue!"

"He can't be," said Dot. "The shell is still
on it."

"So why is he stuffing it in his mouth?"
asked Jabber.

The squirrel ran off.

"Oh no, he's stealing the acorn!" the
detectives cried and ran after him.

When the squirrel stopped, they stopped and watched to see what would happen next.

"What's he doing now?" asked Jabber.

"Digging a hole. Look! He's hiding the acorn."

Jabber stared at Dot. "Maybe he's planting it!"

"Of course!" said Dot. "Our acorn crossed the meadow on squirrel feet."

"And got planted by squirrel feet," said Jabber.

"And grew into the little oak tree," said Dot. "The mystery is solved. We are two clever mouse detectives!"

"Hurray!" shouted Jabber. "Now what will we do?"

"Find another mystery," said Dot.

"But I'm hungry," said Jabber. "First let's go eat some of those leftover clues."

Think and Share

Talk About It Dot and Jabber are detectives. Why are they good at what they do?

1. Use the pictures below to summarize what you learned about seeds.

2. Oak tree seeds, or acorns, are different from maple tree seeds. Tell how.

3. Did you have trouble as you read? What did you do? How did that help?

Look Back and Write What was the answer to the great acorn mystery? Look back at page 99.

Meet the Author and Illustrator

Ellen Stoll Walsh

Ellen Stoll Walsh grew up in a big family. She was one of ten children! It was fun but noisy. She liked to read books to get away from the noise.

Now Ms. Walsh writes books. She cuts paper to make the art. In her books, she tells stories and teaches facts about the world.

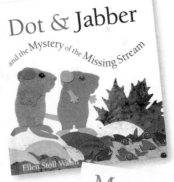

Read more books by Ellen Stoll Walsh.

Water

Our class did an experiment. We observed changes in water. Here's what we did.

1. We put water in a cup.
2. We marked it with a line.
3. We waited one week.
4. We took notes.

We looked at the cup.
We drew another line to
mark the water. The water
went down. Where did it go?
None of us knew.

Our teacher said that the water went into the air. It is there, but we can't see it. This is called evaporation.

We decided to do another experiment. This time we put the water among the plants instead of in the sun. What will happen? We will check for evaporation in a week.

 **Read Together**

How Sentences Begin and End

A **sentence** is a group of words that tells a complete idea. It begins with a **capital letter**. A statement ends with a **period (.)**. A **question** ends with a **question mark (?)**.

Acorns are oak tree seeds**.**

This sentence is a statement. It tells something.

How did this oak tree get here**?**

This sentence is a question. It asks something.

Write Using Sentences

1. Write these sentences. Use capital letters and end marks correctly.

oak trees grow from acorns
how do maple trees grow

· ·

2. Find a statement and a question in *Dot & Jabber and the Great Acorn Mystery.* Write the sentences.

· ·

3. What do you want to know about trees? Write a question. Then answer the question. Use capital letters and end marks correctly.

Let's Talk About

Ideas That Changed the World

Words to Read

goes

kinds

heavy

against

today

Read the Words

The forklift goes back and forth. It lifts all kinds of heavy boxes. It stacks them against the wall. The boxes will be shipped today.

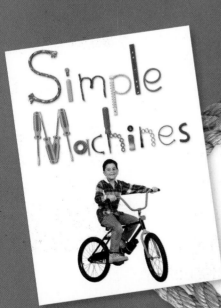

Genre: Expository Nonfiction
Expository nonfiction explains something. The next selection explains how simple machines make work easier.

Simple Machines

by Allan Fowler

How do simple machines help us?

We use machines every day. Machines help make our lives easier.

Some machines, such as lawn mowers and vacuum cleaners, have many parts.

vacuum cleaner

lawn mower

Other machines have few parts. They are called simple machines. Levers, inclined planes, wheels and axles, and pulleys are four kinds of simple machines.

These everyday things are simple machines.

This bottle opener is a kind of lever.
It helps you remove the cap from a bottle.

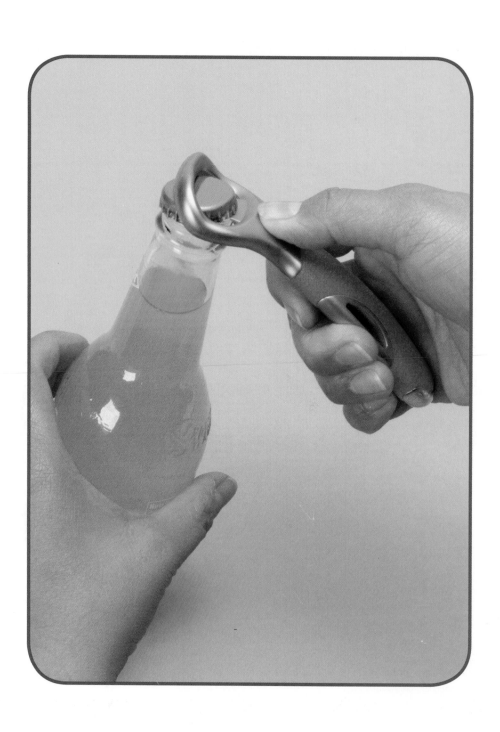

Some levers can help you move a heavy object, such as a rock.

This boy is using a lever called a crowbar.

Push down on one end of a lever. The other end moves up and pushes against whatever you are trying to move.

Have you ever ridden a seesaw?

A seesaw is a kind of lever. One side
goes up, while the other side goes down.

Inclined planes are all around you.

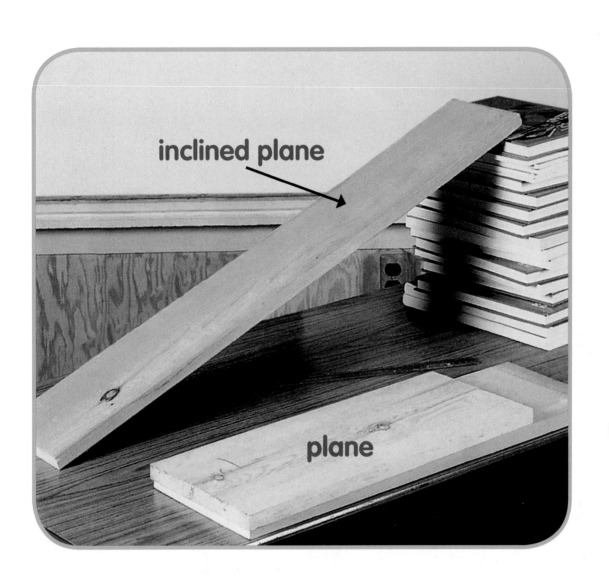

inclined plane

plane

A plane is just a flat surface, like
a wooden board. An inclined plane
is a flat surface that is slanted.

Ramps are inclined planes. It is easier to push a big load up a ramp than to lift it.

A wedge is another kind of inclined plane.

wedge

A wedge can help you cut wood.
When a wedge is hit with a big
hammer, its thin part splits the wood.

Wheels help things go.

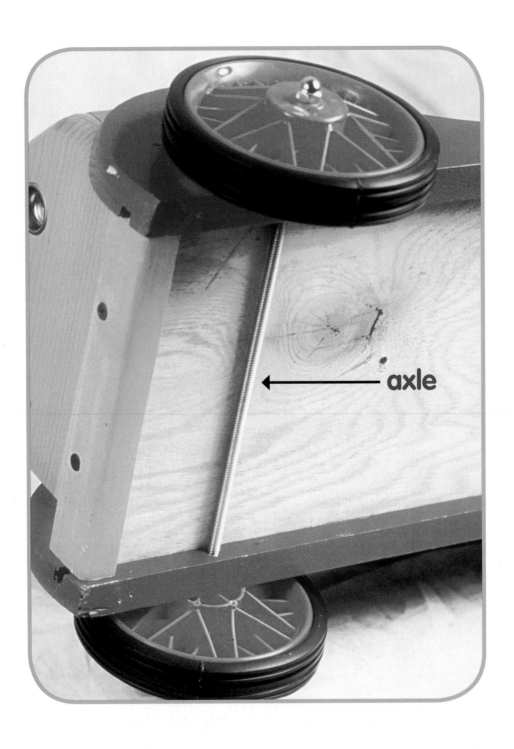

axle

An axle, or rod, connects a pair of
wheels. The axle helps the wheels turn.

Wheels are on bicycles and cars.
It would be very hard to move a bike
or car without wheels.

A pulley helps you lift heavy objects.

pulley

A pulley's rope passes over a small wheel. Pull down on one end of the rope. You can lift a very heavy load tied to the other end.

A pulley can help you raise and lower the flag on a flagpole.

You can even lift the sail on a boat using a pulley.

These children are using two kinds of simple machines. A wheelbarrow is a kind of lever, and it has wheels.

Have you used any simple machines today?

Think and Share

Talk About It Machines can be very simple. Talk about simple machines you use in the classroom.

1. Use the pictures below to summarize what you learned about machines.

2. What is this selection mostly about?

3. Did you stop to sum up after you read about levers before reading on? How did that help you?

Test Practice

Look Back and Write How would you get an inclined plane to help you get a big box onto a truck? Look back at page 124.

Meet the Author
Allan Fowler

Allan Fowler has written many science books for beginning readers. He likes to travel and write about different parts of the world.

Mr. Fowler was born in New York, but he lives in Chicago now. He worked in advertising before he became a writer.

Read more books by Allan Fowler.

Roy's Wheelchair

by Collen Watkins

Roy uses a wheelchair. It has axles and wheels. He goes all around town with it.

Today Roy is going to the toy store.
He uses the ramp to get to the door.

The door is heavy. He pushes against the opener to get in.

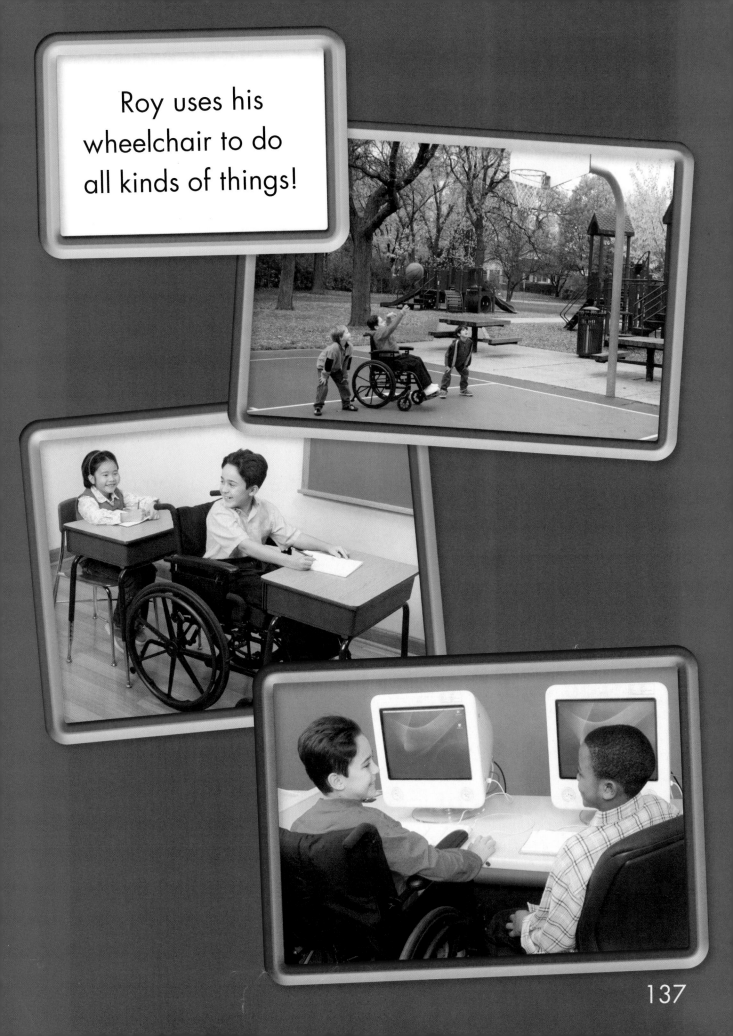

Roy uses his wheelchair to do all kinds of things!

137

Pronouns

A **pronoun** is a word that takes the place of a noun or nouns. The words **he, she, it, I, we, you,** and **they** are pronouns.

The **boy** uses a ramp.   **He** uses a ramp.

The **girl** climbs the stairs.   **She** climbs the stairs.

The **wheel** is round.   **It** is round.

You and I walked.   **We** walked.

Jane, sit down.   **You** sit down.

Chris and Pat lifted it.   **They** lifted it.

Write Using Pronouns

1. Use a pronoun for the words in dark letters. Write the new sentences. Circle the pronouns.

   Sara and Mike used a lever.
   The lever made the work easier.

   ·

2. Find a sentence in *Simple Machines* that uses a pronoun. Write the sentence. Circle the pronoun.

   ·

3. Write about a simple machine. Use pronouns in some of your sentences. Circle the pronouns.

Let's Talk About Ideas That Changed the World

Words to Read

early
learn
science
built
through

Read the Words

Early in life, a man named Mr. Bell liked to learn about science. He later built a machine that sent voices through wires. Do you know the name of that machine?

Alexander Graham **Bell**

Genre: Biography
A biography tells a person's life story. It is written by someone else. Now you will read about the man who invented the telephone, Alexander Graham Bell.

Alexander Graham Bell

by Lola M. Schaefer

Why is Alexander Graham Bell an important person to know?

Alexander Graham Bell was born
in Scotland in 1847. His father was
a famous teacher who taught people
how to speak well.

Time line

born

1847

Scotland

Alexander's mother was deaf.
She was still able to teach him to
play the piano. Alexander was good
at music and science.

Time line

born

1847

The Bell Family
Alexander is on the left.

Alexander was interested in sound. He also liked to invent things. He built a machine that could speak. He also tried to make his dog talk.

 **Time line**

born

1847

**Alexander using
an early invention**

In 1871, Alexander moved to Boston. During the day, he taught deaf students how to speak. At night, he did experiments with sound.

 **Time line**

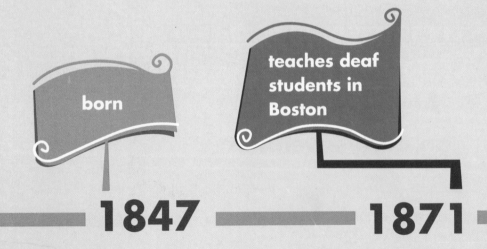

born

teaches deaf students in Boston

1847 — 1871

**Classroom at a school
for the deaf**

Alexander wanted to learn more about electricity. In 1874, he met Tom Watson. Tom knew how electricity worked. They began to work together.

 **Time line**

born

teaches deaf students in Boston

begins work with Tom Watson

1847 **1871** **1874**

Electricity can make sound travel through wires.

Alexander stopped teaching. He did experiments day and night. He and Tom wanted to invent a machine that could send voices from one place to another.

 # Time line

born

teaches deaf students in Boston

begins work with Tom Watson

1847 **1871 1874**

THIS MODEL OF BELL'S FIRST
TELEPHONE IS A DUPLICATE OF THE INSTRU-
MENT THROUGH WHICH SPEECH SOUNDS WERE
FIRST TRANSMITTED ELECTRICALLY, 1875.

**A model of Bell's
first telephone**

On March 10, 1876, Alexander and Tom reached their goal. Alexander spoke to Tom through the first telephone.

 **Time line**

born

teaches deaf students in Boston

begins work with Tom Watson

1847 — **1871** — **1874**

**Alexander Graham Bell
using his telephone**

invents
telephone with
Tom Watson

1876

Alexander and Tom made the telephone better. Soon it could send voices many miles. In 1915, they made the first telephone call across the United States.

 **Time line**

born

teaches deaf students in Boston

begins work with Tom Watson

1847 **1871** **1874**

**The first telephone call
across the United States**

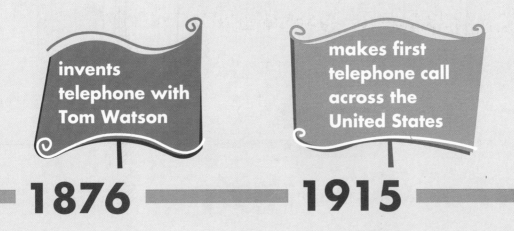

invents
telephone with
Tom Watson

makes first
telephone call
across the
United States

1876   **1915**

Alexander spent his life inventing. He died in 1922. Alexander Graham Bell changed the way people communicate with one another.

Time line

born

teaches deaf students in Boston

begins work with Tom Watson

1847 — **1871** — **1874**

invents telephone with Tom Watson

makes first telephone call across the United States

dies

1876 — **1915** **1922** —

Think and Share

Talk About It What would you say to thank Mr. Alexander Graham Bell for what he did?

1. Use the pictures below to summarize Mr. Bell's life and work.

2. Describe the kind of person Alexander Graham Bell was.

3. How does the time line in this selection help you understand Mr. Bell and his life?

Look Back and Write Look back at page 150. What fantastic thing did Mr. Bell try to do? What do you think happened?

Meet the Author

Lola M. Schaefer

As a child, Lola Schaefer loved to read. "I read every biography in our school library," she says. Now she writes biographies for beginning readers.

Ms. Schaefer says, "Whenever you read a good book, pass it to a friend. Then the two of you can talk about your favorite parts."

Read more books by Lola M. Schaefer.

Inventions

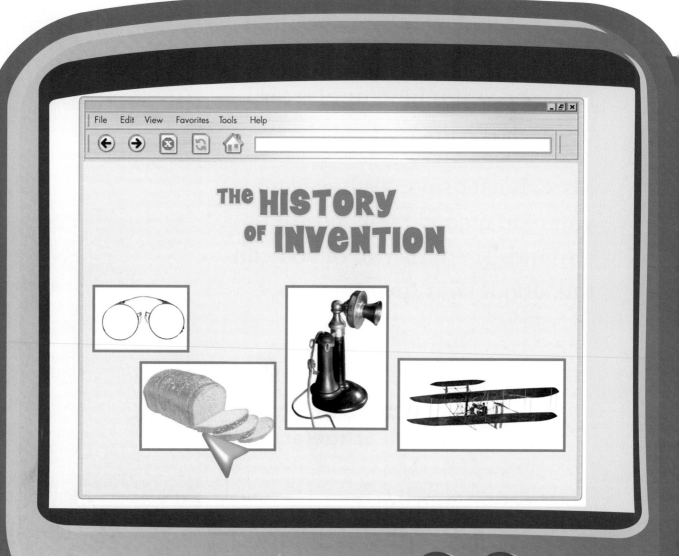

THE **HISTORY** OF **INVENTION**

Maude likes science. She wants to learn more about inventions. So she visits an Internet Web site called The History of Invention. Here's what she sees.

Maude clicks on a picture to learn more.

Sliced bread, invented in 1928

Maude reads about early inventions like eyeglasses and the first airplane ever built. She learns about inventions all through history—even the invention of sliced bread.

Using I and Me

The pronouns **I** and **me** take the place of your name. Use **I** in the subject of a sentence. Use **me** after an action verb. Always write **I** with a capital letter.

I invent things.
My friend helps **me.**

When you talk about yourself and another person, name yourself last. The pronouns **I** and **me** take the place of your name.

Bob and **I** read the instructions.
Ms. Lee helped Bob and **me.**

Write Using I and Me

1. Write these sentences using the correct pronouns.

(I, Me) liked learning about Mr. Bell.
His story gave (I, me) a great idea.
(I, Me) want to invent something.
Jo and (I, me) went to the store.
The teacher helped Jill and (I, me).

· ·

2. Write two sentences that tell what you learned about Alexander Graham Bell. Use the pronouns **I** and **me.**

· ·

3. Write about something you do outside of school. Circle the pronouns **I** and **me.**

Let's Talk About Ideas That Changed the World

Words to Read

brothers
answered
poor
carry
different

172

Read the Words

"How many brothers did Ben Franklin have?" asked Kenji.

"I don't know," answered Carlos, "but I read that his family was poor."

"He liked to carry out many different experiments," added Kate.

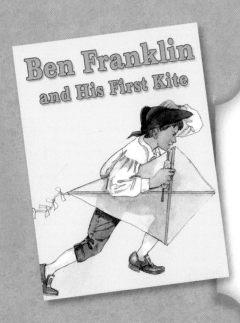

Ben Franklin and His First Kite

Genre: Biography
A biography sometimes tells about only a small part of a person's life. Next you will read about Ben Franklin when he was a boy.

Ben Franklin
and His First Kite

written by Stephen Krensky

illustrated by Bert Dodson

What will Ben do
with his kite?

Ten-year-old Benjamin Franklin was hard at work in his father's candle shop. He was cutting wicks. He carefully laid out each one.

Ben stretched his arms and let out a yawn. Candles could be tall or short, fat or thin, and even different colors. But there was nothing fun about candles for Ben.

"When do you think we'll be done today?"
Ben asked his father.

"Soon enough," his father answered.
"Why? Do you have special plans?"

Ben's father smiled. It was a rare day indeed when Ben did not have a plan in mind.

"Yes," said Ben. "I want to try an experiment at the millpond."

"You'll be swimming, then?" his father asked.

Ben grinned. "Partly," he said.

His father nodded. Ben was a fine swimmer.

That afternoon Ben flew down the streets of Boston. He was headed for home. Along the way he noticed the waves cresting in the harbor. The ships rocked back and forth. That was good, he thought. He needed a strong wind today.

When Ben got to his house, his mother met
him at the door. Inside, two of his sisters were
busy making hasty pudding by the hearth. Ben
had sixteen brothers and sisters.

"Ben," his mother said, "why are you in such
a hurry?"

Ben told her about his plan.

"Since your father approves, I won't keep you," said his mother. "Just be back for supper."

Ben nodded. He ran to get the kite he had made the week before. Then he left the house.

At the millpond a few of Ben's friends had arrived to watch.

"You've picked a poor place to fly a kite," said one.

Ben shrugged. "I'm doing an experiment," he said.

Ben got undressed. He gave his clothes to one of his friends.

"Please carry these to the other side of the pond," he said.

"What are you going to do?" asked the other boys. "Carry the kite while you swim?"

"No," said Ben. "The kite is going to carry me."

"But that kite is nothing special. It's just paper, sticks, and string," said one boy.

"That's true," Ben said. "But you see, the kite isn't the invention. The invention is what I'm going to do with it."

Ben raised the kite in the air. Once the wind had caught and carried it aloft, Ben walked into the water. There he lay on his back, floating.

"I'm going to cross this pond without swimming a stroke," said Ben.

The wind tugged on the kite. The kite string tightened. The water began to ripple at Ben's feet. The kite was pulling him!

The boys whooped and hollered
as Ben glided across the pond. Finally
he reached the other side. The other
boys met him there.

"That was amazing!" said one.

"You crossed the whole pond without
swimming a stroke," said another.

"What will you do next?" they asked.
"Another invention? A different experiment?"
Ben didn't know. But he was sure he would
think of something.

Ben's Great

Ben Franklin

Benjamin Franklin
proved that lightning
is electricity.

Franklin invented
lightning rods. They
are put on houses to
prevent fires caused
by lightning.

Ideas

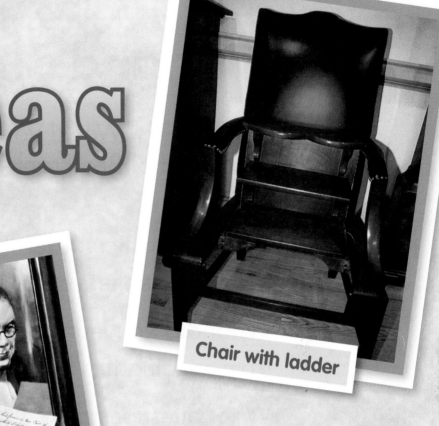
Chair with ladder

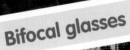
Bifocal glasses

Franklin stove

Think and Share

Talk About It Would you like to have been a friend of Ben Franklin's? Explain.

1. Decide in which order the pictures belong. Use them to retell Ben's story.

2 What did you learn about great ideas from reading this biography?

3. What questions did you ask yourself as you read this selection? How did that help you with your reading?

Look Back and Write Why was a strong wind important to Ben on this day? Look back at page 189 to help you answer.

Stephen Krensky

Stephen Krensky is the author of over seventy books for children! He says, "Writing is hard and fun at the same time."

As a boy Mr. Krensky liked to make up stories. He would pretend he was in big adventures. Today he lives in Massachusetts with his wife and two sons, Andrew and Peter.

Read more books by Stephen Krensky.

Read Together

I Made a Mechanical Dragon

by Jack Prelutsky
illustrated by Peter Sis

I made a mechanical dragon
Of bottle tops, hinges, and strings,
Of thrown-away clocks and unmendable socks,
Of hangers and worn innersprings.
I built it of cardboard and plastic,
Of doorknobs and cables and corks,
Of spools and balloons and unusable spoons,
And rusty old hinges and forks.

It's quite an unusual dragon
It rolls on irregular wheels,
It clatters and creaks and it rattles and squeaks,
And when it tips over, it squeals.
I've tried to control its maneuvers,
It fails to obey my commands,
It bumps into walls till it totters and falls—
I made it myself with my hands!

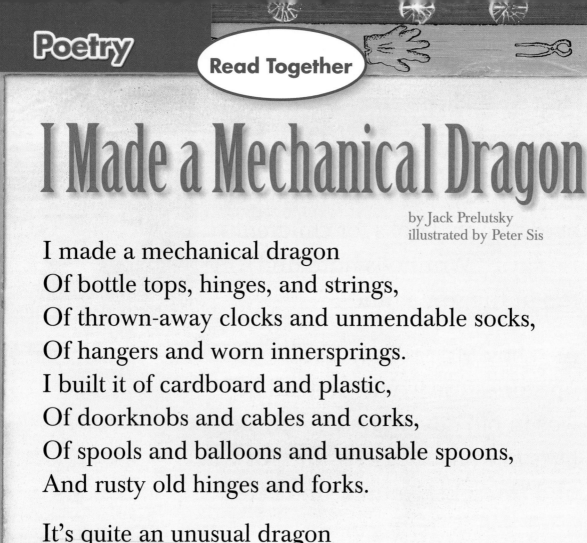

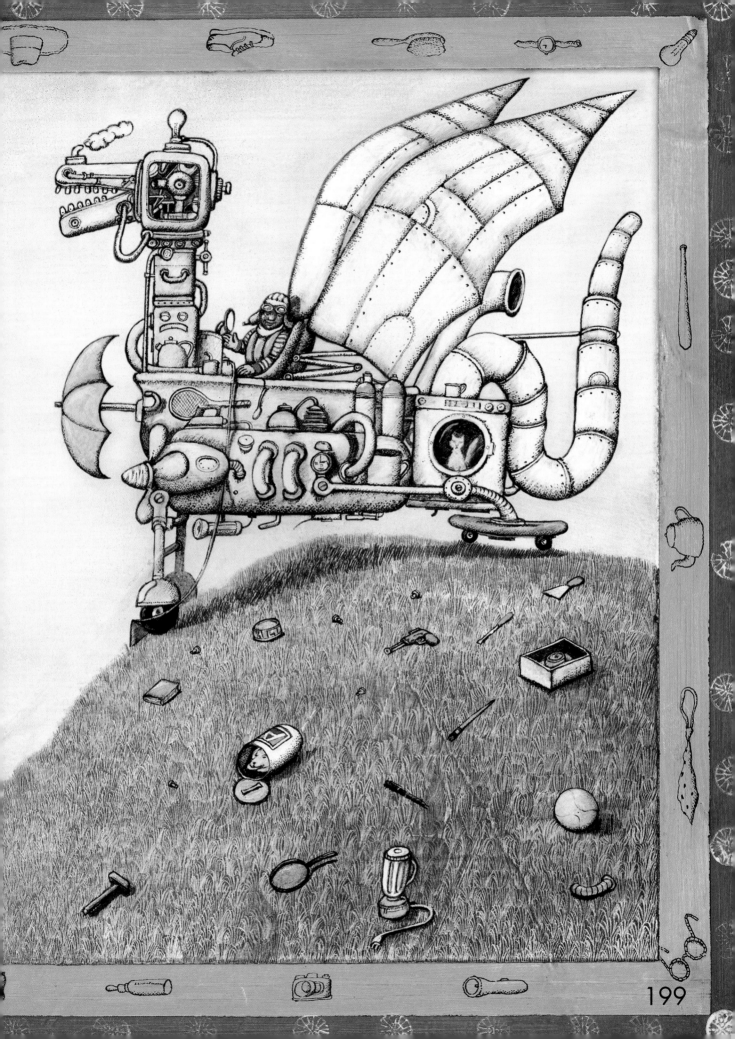

Lighthouse

LIG

by Joan Bransfield Graham
illustrated by Nancy Davis

Oh, Captain of the midnight sky, you stretch your arms and flash your eye across the waves and churning foam to steer me, guide me, safely HOME.

LIGHT HOUSE

Read Together

More About Pronouns

· ·

A **pronoun** can take the place of some words in a sentence. **I, you, he, she, it, we,** and **they** are used in the **naming part** of a sentence. **Me, you, him, her, it, us,** and **them** are used in the **action part**.

· ·

Ben had a kite.   **He** had a kite.

The work was done.   **It** was done.

His friends helped him.   **They** helped him.

They like **Ben**.   They like **him**.

Ben called **his mother**.   Ben called **her**.

Ben saw **Tom and Meg**.   Ben saw **them**.

Write Using More Pronouns

1. Write these sentences. Use pronouns in place of the words in dark letters.

Ben crossed the pond
The wind blew him across.
Ben surprised **his friends**.

· ·

2. Find two sentences in *Ben Franklin and His First Kite* that use pronouns. Write the sentences. Circle the pronouns.

· ·

3. Write sentences about an experiment or a project that you did with your friends. Use pronouns. Circle them.

What's the Big Idea?

connect to
WRITING

Look around your home and school. Find a machine or another idea that makes a big difference in your life. Draw a picture of it. Write how it changes your life.

The Best Idea

connect to
DRAMA

What was the best idea you read about in this unit? Choose the story that tells about the best idea. Act out the story with a friend. Tell how the idea makes a difference.

A Good Result

connect to
SOCIAL STUDIES

Mole did not want his bird to fly. Then Grandad changed Mole's mind. Think about a time you changed your mind. Why was that a good idea? Talk it over with a partner.

I Can Find the Answer

Where can you find the answers to questions?

Right There In the Book

Sometimes the answers are RIGHT THERE in the book. You can put your finger right on the answer.

You might read this text and this question:

Hurray! Today is the 4th of July. My family will go to a party on our block. At night we will see fireworks. They will light up the dark sky.

1 When will the family see fireworks?

○ in the morning

◉ at night

○ the next day

 Look back at the text. The answer is RIGHT THERE.

I Can Find the Answer

In My Head

Sometimes the answers are NOT right there in the text. You must read what the author wrote and use your head. You must FIGURE IT OUT!

You might read this text and this question:

We all went to the park to see the fireworks. Crack! Bang! The sounds were very loud. Then a baby began to cry. She cried very hard!

1 How did the baby feel?

- ○ happy

- ○ cold

- ● afraid

Look at this clue. You can use your head to FIGURE OUT how the baby feels.

Try It!

In the Book

Sometimes the answers are RIGHT THERE in the book. You can put your finger right on the answer.

You might read this text and this question:

Mr. Bear liked lots of foods. He liked to eat bugs. He liked to eat grass. But Mr. Bear's favorite treat was honey. ←

1 **What did Mr. Bear like most?**

○ bugs

○ grass

○ honey

Look back at the text.
The answer is RIGHT THERE.

In My Head

Sometimes the answers are NOT right there in the text. You must read the text and use your head to find the answers. You must FIGURE IT OUT!

You might read this text and this question:

Mr. Bear was looking for food. He saw bees flying into a hive. "Yes!" said Mr. Bear. He knew something good was inside the hive. ← Soon he would eat a good dinner.

1 What will Mr. Bear have for dinner?

○ bees

○ hive

○ honey

Look at this clue. It will help you choose the right answer.

Glossary

Aa

amazing Something that is **amazing** is very surprising. The hero made an **amazing** escape.

axles **Axles** are bars on which wheels turn.

axle

Bb

borrowed If you **borrowed** something, you got it from a person or a place just for a while. I **borrowed** books from the library.

Boston **Boston** is the capital city of Massachusetts, which is a state in the United States.

breath **Breath** is air taken into and sent out of the lungs. Take a deep **breath.**

Cc

communicate To **communicate** is to give and take news and information.

Dd

detectives **Detectives** are police officers or other people who work at solving mysteries.

disagreed If you and a friend **disagreed,** that means both had different ideas.

disagreed

Ee

electricity **Electricity** is a kind of energy that makes light and heat. **Electricity** also runs motors. **Electricity** makes light bulbs shine, radios and televisions play, and cars start.

Ff

famous A **famous** person is one who is well-known and important. The **famous** singer was met by a large crowd.

favorite Your **favorite** thing is the one you like better than all the others. What is your **favorite** flower?

Hh

harbor A **harbor** is an area of water where ships are safe. The boat sailed for the **harbor** when the storm began.

harbor

hasty pudding **Hasty pudding** is mush made of cornmeal.

hearth A **hearth** is the stone or brick floor of a fireplace.

hey **Hey** is a sound you make to get someone's attention.

hurray **Hurray** is what you shout when you are very happy. Give a **hurray** for our team!

hearth

213

Ii

inclined plane An **inclined plane** is a plank or other flat surface placed at an angle and used to move heavy things to a higher place. It is a simple machine.

inclined plane

invention An **invention** is a new thing that someone makes or thinks of. The light bulb was a wonderful **invention.**

Ll

lawn A **lawn** is a piece of land that is covered with grass and near a house. The grass of a **lawn** is usually kept short.

Mm

machines **Machines** are things with moving parts that do work for you. Cars, washers, and computers are **machines.**

meadow A **meadow** is a piece of land where grass grows. There are sheep in the **meadow.**

meadow

million A **million** is a very large number. It is also written 1,000,000.

mystery A **mystery** is something that is hard to understand. It was a **mystery** why the radio started playing in the middle of the night.

Pp

piano A **piano** is a large musical instrument that you sit at and play with your fingers.

potato bug

potato bugs **Potato bugs** are beetles that eat the leaves of the potato plant.

presently **Presently** means at the present time, or now. She is **presently** in first grade.

pulleys **Pulleys** are wheels with ropes that help lift things.

pulley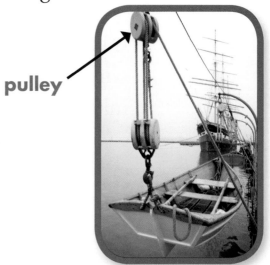

Ss

Scotland **Scotland** is a country north of England.

solve When you **solve** something, you find the answer to it. The detective will **solve** the mystery by using the clues.

solved **Solved** is the past tense of *solve*.

surface A **surface** is the top part or outside of something. The **surface** of the road was very wet after the rain.

surface

Tt

telephone A **telephone** is something you use to talk to people far away. Please answer the **telephone** if it rings.

telephone

tippy-toe **Tippy-toe** means on the tips of your toes. The girl walked **tippy-toe** so that she would not wake her baby brother.

tippy-toe

Uu

usually If something **usually** happens, it happens very often or almost all the time. We **usually** eat dinner at six o'clock.

Vv

vacuum A **vacuum** cleaner is a machine you can use to clean rugs, curtains, and floors.

vacuum

Tested Words

Tippy-Toe Chick, Go!

along
behind
eyes
never
pulling
toward

Mole and the Baby Bird

door
loved
should
wood

Dot & Jabber and the Great Acorn Mystery

among
another
instead
none

Simple Machines

against
goes
heavy
kinds
today

Tested Words

Alexander Graham Bell

built
early
learn
science
through

Ben Franklin and His First Kite

answered
brothers
carry
different
poor

Acknowledgments

Text

Page 14: *Tippy-Toe Chick, Go!* by George Shannon, illustrations by Laura Dronzek. Text copyright © 2003 by George W. B. Shannon. Illustrations copyright © 2003 by Laura Dronzek. Used by permission of HarperCollins Publishers.

Page 48: *Mole and the Baby Bird* by Marjorie Newman, illustrated by Patrick Benson. Text copyright © 2002 by Marjorie Newman. Illustrations copyright © 2002 by Patrick Benson. Reprinted by permission of Bloomsbury Publishing.

Page 80: Excerpt from *Dot & Jabber and the Great Acorn Mystery*, copyright © 2001 by Ellen Stoll Walsh, reprinted by permission of Harcourt, Inc. This material may not be reproduced in any form or by any means without the prior written permission of the publisher.

Page 114: From *Simple Machines* by Allan Fowler. © 2001 Children's Press®. A Division of Grolier Publishing Co., Inc. All rights reserved. Published simultaneously in Canada. Reprinted by permission.

Page 144: *Alexander Graham Bell* by Lola M. Schaefer. Copyright © 2003 by Capstone Press. Reprinted by permission.

Page 174: From *Ben Franklin and His First Kite*. Text copyright © 2002 by Stephen Krensky. Illustrations copyright © 2002 by Bert Dodson. Reprinted with permission of Aladdin Paperbacks, Simon & Schuster Children's Publishing Division. All rights reserved.

Page 198: "I Made A Mechanical Dragon" from *The Dragons are Singing Tonight* by Jack Prelutsky, illustrated by Peter Sis. Text copyright © 1993 by Jack Prelutsky. Illustrations copyright © 1993 by Peter Sis. Used by permission of HarperCollins Publishers.

Page 200: "Lighthouse" from *Flicker Flash*. Text copyright © 1999 by Joan Bransfield Graham. Illustrations copyright © 1999 by Nancy Davis. Reprinted by permission of Houghton Mifflin Company. All rights reserved.

Illustrations

Cover: Daniel Moreton

14-33 Laura Dronzek

36-41 Viviana Garofoli

44-73 Patrick Benson

198 Peter Sis

Photographs

Every effort has been made to secure permission and provide appropriate credit for photographic material. The publisher deeply regrets any omission and pledges to correct errors called to its attention in subsequent editions.

Unless otherwise acknowledged, all photographs are the property of Scott Foresman, a division of Pearson Education.

Photo locators denoted as follows: Top (T), Center (C), Bottom (B), Left (L), Right (R), Background (Bkgd).

7 ©Xavier Bonghi/Getty Images

8 (Bkgd) ©Bill Ross/Corbis, (L) ©Xavier Bonghi/Getty Images

9 (CR) ©Ross Whitaker/Getty Images, (BR) ©Bettmann/Corbis

10 ©Andy Roberts/Stone/Getty Images

11 (BL) Getty Images, (T) Ghislain & Marie David de Lossy/Image Bank/Getty Images

44 ©Martin Harvey/Gallo Images/Corbis

45 (TL, BL) AP/Wide World Photos, (CR) ©Chinch Gryniewicz/Ecoscene/Corbis

103 ©Benjamin M. Walsh

110 ©Peter Samuels/Corbis

111 (B) ©Dennis MacDonald/PhotoEdit, (T) ©Royalty-Free/Corbis, (CR) ©Derek P. Redfearn/Getty Images

112 Getty Images

113 ©Comstock, Inc.

114 (CL) ©Comstock, Inc., (BC) Corbis

115 (Bkgd) ©Ross Whitaker/Getty Images, (BC) ©Comstock, Inc.

116 (CR) Corbis, (B) ©Comstock, Inc.

117 ©Nance S. Trueworthy

119 ©Tony Freeman/PhotoEdit

120 ©Michelle D. Bridwell/PhotoEdit

122 (TR) ©Royalty-Free/Corbis, (TL) ©Kayte M. Deioma/PhotoEdit, (B) ©Dennis MacDonald/PhotoEdit

123 Stock Boston

124 (T) ©David Young-Wolff/PhotoEdit, (B) ©Bonnie Kamin/PhotoEdit

125 ©David Forbert/SuperStock

126 Unicorn Stock Photos

Acknowledgments

127 (T) Affordable Photo Stock/Francis & Donna Caldwell, (B) ©Royalty-Free/Corbis

128 Stock Boston

129 (TL) ©Mary Kate Denny/PhotoEdit, (BR) ©Laurence Monneret/Getty Images

130 Stock Boston

131 (TL, BR) ©Tom Stewart/Corbis, (TR) ©Jennie Woodcock/Reflections Photolibrary/Corbis, (BL) ©George Shelley/Corbis

133 ©Comstock, Inc.

139 ©David Forbert/SuperStock

140 ©Royalty-Free/Corbis

141 (BL, TL) ©Bettmann/Corbis, (TR) Reuters/Corbis

142 ©Bettmann/Corbis

145 Corbis

147 ©E.O. Hoppe

149 ©A. G. Bell National Historic Site

151 ©Bettmann/Corbis

153 Corbis

155 ©Gordon Osmundson/Corbis

157, 159, 161 ©Bettmann/Corbis

163 Corbis

166 (L, CC, CL) Hemera Technologies, (CR) Wright State University Library

167 Hemera Technologies

169 Corbis

170 ©Ariel Skelley/Corbis

171 (Bkgd) ©ML Sinibaldi/Corbis, (BL) Terry W. Eggers/Corbis, (TR) ©Jennie Woodcock/Corbis, (C) ©Richard Cummins/Corbis

194 (TL) ©Stock Montage/SuperStock, (BL) North Wind Picture Archives, (CR) The Granger Collection, NY

195 (CL) ©Bettmann/Corbis, (B) The Granger Collection, NY, (TR) ©Jeff Greenberg

197 ©Stephen Krensky

204 (CL) ©David Young-Wolff/PhotoEdit, (BL) ©Xavier Bonghi/Getty Images, (Bkgd) ©Bill Ross/Corbis

207, 209 ©Larry Williams/Corbis

209 ©Larry Williams/Corbis

210 Unicorn Stock Photos

211 ©Ariel Skelley/Corbis

213 (TR, CL) Getty Images

214 ©David Young-Wolff/PhotoEdit

215 Getty Images

216 (BR) Stock Boston, (CL) ©Royalty-Free/Corbis

217 ©Royalty-Free/Corbis

218 Getty Images

219 Corbis

221 ©Nance S. Trueworthy

222 ©Bettmann/Corbis

Glossary

The contents of this glossary have been adapted from *First Dictionary*. Copyright © 2000, Pearson Education, Inc.

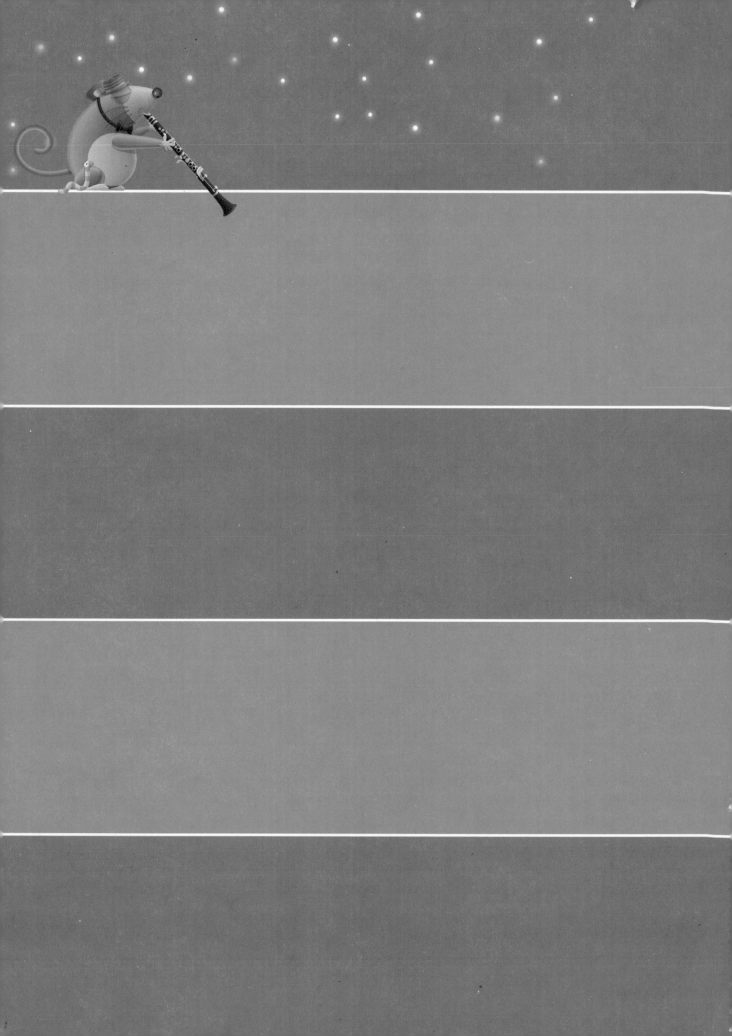